Gallery Books
Editor Peter Fallon

THEN THE HARE

Michelle O'Sullivan

THEN
THE HARE

Gallery Books

Then the Hare
is first published
simultaneously in paperback
and in a clothbound edition
on 23 November 2023.

The Gallery Press
Loughcrew
Oldcastle
County Meath
Ireland

www.gallerypress.com

ISBN 978 1 91133 866 6 *paperback*
      978 1 91133 867 3 *clothbound*

A CIP catalogue record for this book
is available from the British Library.

Then the Hare receives financial assistance
from the Arts Council of Ireland.

Contents

for Evelyn and Hugh

Welcome, Stranger

It seems the first in weeks —
actual sunlight on the table,
a strip so wide you could
warm your hands in it.

And this sudden glee that it's
you who comes to mind:
'Welcome, stranger, to this place
where Joy doth sit on every bough.'

Catching the Sun By Its Tail

Insofar as catching
the sun by its tail
I'm afraid I couldn't —

having had words with goad
I tried allure, induce, made
attempts via croon

and court, even tried lullaby
variations before I cast
a hook with winnow

and went as far
as thinking I could see it slice,
could swear the silver

line of it sheered,
cutting blue as it went
the pinked open air.

Notation

We're fields apart.
Sky
and blue over the river.

Something about the light
or blind
bends along the coast.

Everything about direction,
the going to
or from.

And the mountain ahead,
I thought it
like a licked thumb.

As If Already

The breathless getting dark and less warm
sorrows bedding down and a moon cutting
its teeth that will later make visible half-
moons of goatskin beneath the mantel's
clock piece.

Less than a month ago there was the frost
and sky resembling galvanize, dips of cold
pushing air — yet here we are, as if already
a world away, yellow lifting green
from hedge lines.

Grassfire

The road's battered hedge lifts to a new green.
Less distinct: cars, bird noise, a voice that carries
and is sealed with a door closing. Cold and after
cold, sparks from a chimney's throat, fog unable
to keep a foothold at the river's approach.

Here are the beasts that stood in darkened sheds
only days ago, trace-work of blood and scars
on their de-horned heads not fresh but visible.
Bound to no season, white sunlight trembles
at the small wave — I almost envy them.

Moor

Think of all the motion of the waves, you said,
speaking of home as a vague island,
an unapproachable blue,
offshore and remote;

the half-submerged rocks
and rocks set deep in the unseen
belly down sleeping the sleep
of the drowned

and I said, even if it were the sea we aimed for
there was the quay's tug and pull
as if not wanting to lose distance
from our heel.

Snug as a boat's cold engine,
there was the inherent silence of clouds
as they made their way to dissolve
over the Atlantic.

Light Twice

Unlike the rest
of your timid crew

you appear at the top
of the drive

and have a good clean
of a back foot

while equally having
a good look around,

morning opened
but turning brighter,

all the time
sun inching

toward being
overhead,

unsure if you've
made me,

statue that I am
fenced behind glass;

it is the blithe of you
that I want to carry

for the rest of the day,
the evening.

I want to carry it
for weeks and months.

That Heron

I walked the field again
half-rounding its hill
a slow rise of a climb
downing to the riverline,

I wanted to see again
that heron, then the hare —
the way it happened when
you were last here,

I'd pointed at the same
time you'd said look.

Quieted, as if trying to figure
or refigure a tune, I knew it
wasn't what was here
but what was left.

From the Bridge

A new copse, part-upholstered trunks
effected bronze in the later light,
sidelong branches almost holding
but for an arm's sway

and over the road the small fields
and the small river islands
and the river touching the curve
of their jawlines.

Fire Season

The house empty but not abandoned
and an August bright resolved to burn
for the possibility of another hour
softens the stalks of gladioli that have overshot
a boundary wall. They are tall and only
green. I remember bedding them,
and the cold. I remember the raw silk of frost
and the minor galaxy of light that burned
from the front room; the late afternoon
kindness, winter's version. Is it the gladioli,
not one of them in bloom, that draw me
to that winter, this fidelity to bulbs
in a muzzle of cold with the dark coming on?
There was no doubt (it never occurred)
they couldn't bloom.

What Must the Postman Think

The deadheading put off, having reasoned
time might proffer a later bloom

and the storm-split trunk, quite possibly the root,
of a decades old lilac that I find hard to look at.

What is it then —
beyond a misjudged call,

one bird's note with another's answer?
What I'm looking for isn't what I'm looking at.

A week now and it's almost comical
how I've tried to avoid them,

and the shears and axe
I'd placed beside the letterbox.

Double Takes

1

We'd reached a spot beside Ross Strand.
Tide further than imagined, its distance
was so remote that I doubted water
had been here at all.

There were remnants of boat rope.
Dead silence in noughts.
Cold that had become cognate
to my mother tongue.

2

Cask half-split and a lived-in depth
with its new shoots of grass,
it looks as if the warmed-up air
has begun to move

even to its darker parts. Mask slipped,
I almost don't recognize the river, width
and breadth an earthy air, plum-blue ruts
and untouched ambers.

3

In Siena a woman stands not quite at an edge;
there's the curtain she peers from and the window
she's affixed to, her gaze locked on a pomegranate
and caterpillar.

A double take and this mixed sense of being
taken in and fooled, the spread of her hand gentling dark,
reaching for something
like life in the real.

The Going (1)

The sea's black highlighted by the waves
rolled out white. I crossed the pier and moved
up the recently tarmacked path, a sleepy line
abutting land and water —

and the cry came from nowhere, somewhere
further beyond the rows of coastal houses, the cliffs,
as if a director had staged a child and kept
her curtained behind the scenes —

and the tide kept going and going out,
a pair of strays ran parallel to live voltage,
a lack of crisis stared back from the face
of a pedigree bull.

With

small hours and grasses
green turned resting,

the days worn cloth
scrubbed to a soft dark

as if by hands that have
been and are now done,

and this modest reach
of a field's cosmic hides.

The Round Stone

That long ago, how was it only ourselves that day in May?
Unsure who was more contrary, you with your teething
and my grandfather's tricky combination that boiled down
to not always saying what he felt or wanted.

Naturally I thought him messing when he told me
where I'd find the scythe and the round stone that would clean
its film of rust; not a few rushes, there was a whole meadow
that needed cutting.

We managed. Day followed night. The world turned.
No single thing could be or would be made different.

Passage

We return to beds that may have been made
before a crisis brought us together.

Too many stars. I wish I hadn't looked up
when I'd gone out to close the gates.

Lavender and begonia turn dark in wide pots.
The dog answers another dog with a deeper bark.

Sleepless, I pitch gift and purchase.
I circle benevolent like the number eight.

This quiet
knowing so many things I don't.

Half the Portrait

Semi-darkness through the house,
blues and maybe the fog of blues

altered by windows that yield
alternate versions of stars;

orange by black with the stove
and its closed door, the cheek

of a cup touched
by the warm of a teapot;

and the bedrooms upstairs
nearly as dark as the sheds.

Scale

I wake to the part of your face driven quiet,
to light rending dark at the crossroads,

uncertain if I said before or after
that I'd wanted to learn Portuguese,

that sure it was easier to trust
this often said difficult tongue

and because I can't explain the draw
of these nighttime visions

I draw them closer
like a garment.

The Last Conversation We Never Had

Listening for you
and the swifts that have made a thorough-

fare between the back of the house
and its outbuilding.

Moon immaculate as the sun was hours ago
means I can almost see thistle and whin.

Intimate as it gets, wind plays with the roof
but no sounds bristle the sheds.

A Fact, Keats Said, Is Not a Truth Until You Love It

After a storm you'd scavenge the treeline for kindling.
I'd watch the dark draw its hand around your face.
And then the light.

Between the few sods you tuck in at the rear and one
balancing the middle you fret the heel of a hand
to another.

It's how you build the nest. When did it dawn that this
was and wasn't how you got the fire going. I can't
remember when I first loved this.

Your Ladies

I didn't like to ask because I didn't like to explain
the contentment they've infected me with,

calved and the mother stood nearly still, an older
calf looking to nudge the newest;

how had I come to think that I knew the humour
and almost came to depend on hearing

them breathe at night and can it, does it
rationalize my missing them?

You brought it all down a peg or two when you said
they'd be returning, they were only on holidays in Swinford.

Poem with a Line Borrowed from Marguerite Duras

Laid bare after the cattle were moved and the gates closed
there was what the light was doing with the field
and the heaped stones in its middle.

I hadn't been able to see the flowering realized
so late in summer, yellow-purples making subtle
blues of grit still browning under sun,

what'd been initially thought bleak and what's
grown, *a single look to stand for a whole love* —
is this it?

Missing It

The rain while we didn't talk stopped falling
and the river I couldn't see was a miniature
black streak. Part of me inside the low reclined
to take it in while another version had me shaking
this globe, cloud following cloud following cloud
and so on, all these sentiments containing
sediment, dirt, crust.

The Going (2)

I don't expect you because of the rain.
And because we've quarrelled my daughter
still sleeps or pretends to sleep while I nurse
the cool-quiet of the kitchen.

There's the grimace at the sound of your jeep
and the wakefulness I lack today. You're already
unscrewing bolts before my shoes are laced
and when I'm beside you at the wall

I do nothing but watch flakes of post-box red
loosen to the pavement. I can't say I know
what's been said or what we're saying
as we carry the piece of ironwork to the shed

and I'm almost confused with how we go,
how we're going — first you're facing me
walking backward and in a single turn
there's the black of your rain-wet back.

Though I've asked, you won't stop or stay
for tea and it's happened that quick —
I'm trying to remember how we stood there
ever since.

Kitty's Place

Learning the road I sometimes slow after the incline
that bends, a few fields above the house. It's quiet
in the sense that people say it can be a quiet road.
Smaller, and a mixed bunch

that like to crowd the hedge, I see Lavin's bucks
before the muscle of Reid's Charolais. At night a green-
yellow glow dulls from batteries that keep the fences

ticking. Maybe a habit that I've taken to coming in
by the well where a line of sycamore and whitethorn
spear long and shorts of deadwood; often I try
to picture Kitty, features strained or softened

against so much sky, how she must've admired them
full bloom, when it was her place and she ran a sweet
shop from one of the front rooms.

Days

When I'd rather stand in
and out of sun as I strip
the wall dresser's layer
after layer,

would rather feel the spit
and burn from stray
splatter of white
spirits,

would rather this dialect
of plain speak even if
it's only square inches
of unaffected grain.

The View from Scurmore

The light tender but cool
and a dense smell of tree
roots peat-thick.

Beyond the river
where seals have
downed themselves

to sand and stone
and one another, cloud
chases May's cache.

Near and far pegs of yellow,
esters of green and grey;
an almost hard silence

save the wind in breaths
like the punctuated sleep
of a sick child.

Delft

A piece of ash pulled from a scarf and held briefly,
and an insistence on things being what they weren't.
There was the argument and the demand

to be hushed. As if disregarding the abovesaid there were
rents: a faint but distinct splitting followed by a fainter
distinct splitting.

Outside it was as dark as the light. The herd
still visible in the middle field, all of them laying
quiet, foretold the coming rain.

A disorder in the scrapping of shapes
meant that it didn't matter whether it was noon or six.
A Tuesday or a Saturday.

Coordinates

Do you remember the brief happiness at being
away, the city entirely familiar and foreign
in the way cities can be, streets we never quite
lost ourselves on, bridges crossed to go
only so far and doubling sideways to cross another?
Maybe the idea that anything was in the mix
urged us into a freewheel; days were ice-bright,
north winds came unclothed. There were clues,
a litter of falsetto notes that you'd let fall
and I looked at them after, everything recollected
with an urban dark, like a woman stood at a particular
building awed by the din and glow of its stories;
in each of them I could see you arranging
for an order. It startled — that I knew and didn't
know your face. There was our last day. We'd left
an exhibition late. The outside and its field of steps
were burnished to a high purple-black. We sat into them
and, for the first time in days, a calm claimed you.
It felt of saltwater. Of a swimmer at rest
before circling back.

A Winter in Milan

1

I can't place the hour
unsure if it's night
or the cliché of another dusk

there's the snow-glide of taxis
and the snow and the illusion
of warmth

warmth in the pleasurable
strings of lights yellowing
necklines of shopfronts

yesterday when there was
rain and no one stopped
to look

the surprise
when I saw the pashmina
thrown open

the June green
the smile
a bouquet's rumour

as if the act
alone were spark
enough

a reminiscence
that satisfying
and I caught

myself smiling
pleased for having
seen the simple act

and when you asked me what
what you meant was
what was I smiling at

and I couldn't include you
not for lack
but no heart

left for you
and so you abruptly
left the table for the queue

and I watched you become
part of the snake
making its way

out the door
and I remember
thinking I hope

I have lost you
thinking what had become
as familiar as —

it was unfortunate
that you didn't keep going
keep coming back

there was that
stillness
yesterday

2

I faltered over phrases
to tell the taxi driver I needed to stop
get out here

and eventually I got out halfway
up the street because
of traffic

and the exhilaration
of the cold
an almost instant satisfaction

I knew if I turned
I'd miss the feeling
of feeling the snow

and I already knew
what you looked like
receding

the quick repeat
the few seconds
the words I spoke

before I got out
I'll be as quick
and you interjected

looking the other way
how long in retrospect
the timing of your response

some things are and aren't
an eternity a recognition
an instant satisfaction

and maybe it had to do
with the sense of the cold
the sense of snow

the errand I wanted
to execute alone
was opposite

instinctually I knew
that this wasn't
what I was looking at

3

When I returned
the bed-concealed
shape of you

the corner of the room
shallower or deeper
than I'd remembered

I closed the door
much softer
than when I'd opened it

and looked for the hotel bar
the place was old and outside
the city

there was only the dining room
and they stopped serving
long ago

a mix of English and Italian
from the man at reception
who welcomed me

to purchase *vino*
who was happy to let me sit
in *sala da bello*

and the troubling then
to find the power
for the lights

how long he took
yet it all seemed to fit
the grand of the room

the masks on the wall
the shadows of the masks
on the wall

I felt free
does this explain how
the dark felt comforting

I left when lights came
on and carried the dark
to bed

I once saw a mourner inhale
as if her life depended on it
I think it was a little like that

4

The snow was gone
the day after that
and though it didn't rain

until we got to the airport
it could have been
raining all morning

and no one would have
spoken about it
don't we always talk

about the weather
I stood into the glare
arrivals departures

yellow as the whins
and thought of the watch
left behind for repair

even though I had
the written promise
to have it couriered

I thought of the broken
crystal its tree-like design
that grew where I accidently

hit it against the doorjamb
the nights I'd rub my thumb
along the offshoots

looking maybe for new
ones even though I might
have known better

sometimes in the morning
I'd find the ticking
under the pillowcase

it was like listening
to a song
that knows your blood

and maybe it was a reminder
that some things
were still working

what told me
this was
too

5

I daydream
let the rhythm slow
enough to hear

other sounds emerge
a frustration of horns
doors opening

an inhalation commencing
an untouched-up song
a door closing

I follow another version
follow streets
go this way for that

similar strings of lights
are warm against
a similar fall of snow

a shopkeeper sings
backup to a recording
of Patsy Cline

and I sit on a bench
to wait the song
out

but I keep walking too
I keep walking until I can't hear
the rise and fall anymore

At the Surface

Venus changes from evening star to morning star
and almost surpasses earth every 584 days.
There is that realignment.

Of earth's sister or evil twin, a decided leaning
to the former, dusk-concealed road yet this far
away she's sometimes seen midday;
backlit by the sun and all her brightness fades.

An international convention has decreed all features
and formations on the planet be named after women.
Apparently there is a shortage of goddesses
in their databases.

No latitude for lightfall and, phrase-exact perhaps,
the terminator was devised to express the divide
between day and night; a little like love, brutal as that.

Over the Estuary

Marram sharpens the dunes. And there's a roar
that keeps coming inland. A pair of water spaniels
sprint to turn into a bend where sand spires
and knocks decibels to such a point.

Because he thinks we're going swimming my dog
runs until he realizes I'm not there and loops back
to find where I've gone; wind has grass stood straight.
From here we sea-watch a while through its tips.

Over the estuary cattle have been taken in for winter
and I try to find the nearest edge where land meets
water. Years ago I wrote of starfall here, but it was
actually starfall over Bartragh.

That was the year everything froze. Roads closed and pipes
ceased to flow. There were fires in every working fireplace
and children worried about sleighs and rooftops.
That was the year I held fire, until I didn't.

On Business

1

I'm out walking the dog and he's walking toward
a back field to check on one of his horses. Not quite
neighbours, we occasionally salute when inclined
to recognize one another. Watching him just now,
the set-but-carefree ways, the jacket at his shoulder,
everything made more casual with the stream
of his hi-lo whistle; the figure he cuts moves the air
as if he were descending into a panel painting.
It's still Monday. A warm current threads the winter
evening. I hear the gate shut with sincerity.

2

I'm out walking the dog and she's walking toward
a back field to check on one of her horses. Not quite
neighbours, we occasionally salute when inclined
to recognize one another. Watching her just now,
the set-but-carefree ways, the jacket at her shoulder,
everything made more casual with the stream
of her hi-lo whistle; the figure she cuts moves the air
as if she were descending into a panel painting.
It's still Monday. A warm current threads the winter
evening. I hear the gate shut with sincerity.

3

I'm out walking the dog and they're walking toward
a back field to check on one of their horses. Not quite
neighbours, we occasionally salute when inclined
to recognize one another. Watching them just now,
the set-but-carefree ways, the jacket at their shoulder,
everything made more casual with the stream
of their hi-lo whistle; the figure they cut moves the air

as if they were descending into a panel painting.
It's still Monday. A warm current threads the winter
evening. I hear the gate shut with sincerity.

Inking the Time-stop

There were water sounds and night sounds and the tarred
road with no one on it, trees blue without leaves and winds
that'd pressed past bend and gable end

                                                  when suddenly
everything became lit with the dog's sole bark and I said
to your quiet self on the other end of the line that it's like
a tuning fork looking for pitch.

Not Everything Violent Is Irreversible

Thinking her dead I knelt where flag met grass.
Her still face, one eye open that held a blue
and white piece of sky, that small.

Despite the dog circling I didn't hesitate
taking her into my hands until she blinked,
and startled, took breath again.

Winded or stunned, how long had she lain there?
And the singular moment, it can only have been
minutes that we stayed;

later, when I'd gone out the road and up a steeple
of forestry, there were spurs and correspondences
augmenting the trees.

Vixen

I wish I hadn't shown you the mother
and her cubs as they ran their fox-reds
over the road to find temporary shelter
in the hedge.

Every time I spoke with you after
I wanted to tell you about nights ago
before the moon was fully full,
how it was balmy, and windless.

What had I been doing when I heard
the laughing? And the quick succession
of gunshots that'd made me think the air
had gone black-pink?

I wanted to tell you that when I stood
outside the house there were empty sweet
packets blowing and blown into
the side of the road.

Singing Myself to Sleep

not a soul the window left open
and the song of the dog and the wind
and the wind and the nightjar

and the nightjar and the clock
and the clock in the other room
and the clock packed to a box last year

and the sound of that dark
and the sound of the outside dark
and the sound of not another soul

only the nightjars and the rain
and the rain coming down
and coming down the gutter

and coming down the gravel
down the drive down the tarmac
down to pools

shallow but subtle disturbances
the emergence of halves
this side to that

the dew and light
the juncture of crossable
and uncrossable paths

Swift

Even before you were late you were looked for.
The space above the trees grew larger.

Not so much a design or an architecture;
a hole that didn't know stasis, it widened

and gaped.

A Housekeep

The same doe is moving toward long windows
that have always allowed morning
to ease itself down on the kitchen table
and your bone-china cup.

And maybe like me she wonders where you've gone
or when you'll be back; we weren't there to see
the removal men remove your life's contents
and, at the last, your cast-iron heifer and calf.

Outscoring distance and discord, here's this lustre
of sill and grass still wet that's coming to chime
a late summer morning, dew almost as visible
as the doe's face against glass.

A Winter Pasture

Of the hares one left a trail from a limp backfoot
and even with the set of frost
I asked if you heard the estuary-static,

not quite enmeshed
was how I tried to phrase the violent
but sometimes tacit way river meets sea wall.

You nodded at an upstairs window where
a woman was drawing curtains. I'd seen the stoop
of her the night before and the night

before that and because she stared
through the glass I'd guessed her hands were
pressed to the heat of a radiator.

Coming down the road by the cemetery,
the far-off lights of the town were with us temporarily.
It felt an enormous cold.

The field fronting our house was made
tidy with dark and there was nothing left
of the trail we'd seen starting out.

Nephin would be obscured till morning. What affection
had me thinking we'd just been to the edge
of this world and back?

Totem

after Roderic O'Conor

You bear a resemblance almost as natural
as the glow that's come to meet the shadow

and even though there isn't a hint of cold the red
of your hands lifts the red fabric at your shoulders;

figure the innocence touching the figure of grief
that isn't behind or in front of you, yet.

An Ample Zero

I don't think they mean to dominate the scene, the pair
roughed out by the boats. There's the look of Brando
to one of them in *On the Waterfront* and maybe that's
because I hear him shout *some fucking integrity.*

Cloud here, cloud there, all the bitters of seaweed
mixed with turfsmoke. I think to skirt them as best
I can, to yield toward the night-lit sea, the cliffs, seems
a safer bet.

As in any argument there's always one who walks.
Unfixed as a random star, I think, when he's crossed
my path. His shot-in-distance obscenities don't calcify
any air.

Reading the Scene

When they leave her
out of the trailer

she's charged
with a stillness

as if conducting
her way of being

from the ground
up,

and because every-
thing was backlit

over an hour ago
what had been

accentuated
has a more solid

feel, an older
growth if possible;

not so much
as a whirr,

the stream, the fields,
the tide necking

closer to the whins,
quiet breeding

this quiet
as if to recognize

the bolt, and every-
where signalling

it's okay,
come as you are.

A Different Kind

They're taken to more sheltered spots
while the few bucks busy themselves
with shortened stalks of thistle.

Looking in on the expectant one,
we've watched her sidle from the field's slope
and she's that close there's the blonde-

white of her eyelashes. No dark, and no
stars. We're warm in the summer night.
And unharmed.

Blue on Blue

I hadn't seen you, not fully summer and the shed door
flung to thickened and thickening green and bloom marking
the boundary between your field and mine; I only heard
the gate needing oil.

What compelled, stayed as I was, to watch the careful tread
as you overstepped the rise to come roundabout and side
with the pregnant animal; you stood for that long
you put your hands in your pockets.

And I don't know that I'd made the note yet that I'd remember
this or the mild heat, the hawthorn's lime-whites, the blue-on-blue
roughed overhead. And I don't know that I thought of tenderness
or suffering until you laid the width of your palm to her hip

and let it rest there. After you left, almost quieter than when
you'd arrived, I wanted to get up, move. Break something.
What mattered and what of before this?
And my lost faiths? And what now?

Entropy

There was the smallness of stone on the mountain
and between rain a sometimes sun.

Closer, as if askance from the lawn and hill, there was
a hedged road that allowed cars a disappear into.

There was the kettle quieting after a spell on the boil,
minor particulars, a kitchen's this-and-that sonics:

spoon-tapped cup, dulled teeth on a breadknife,
the sole clock with its slowed mismatched tocks.

There was that sweet-but-not balm of night's previous
fire, of wet tealeaves, pinched-loose tobacco.

And the deeper shapes when the blue room
was still blue, nothing yet defeated or yellowed.

The Wide Sound

The red of a berry
reddening the green
of a tree that darkens
the blue of the lawn;

the song of fingers
running stone and brick
nowhere going nowhere
and glad to be alone;

the house almost
lacquered black
but for the lamp
and its gold thread;

unloveliness half-repaired,
there's a cheek to the door:
is that you, spring,
on the other side?

For a Stranger

I have made the tea and shy-burnt toast
while temporarily losing a self in the skyline.

Sun appears for exactly that long
you might stand in it and become warm.

What needed water has been watered,
what needed feeding has been fed.

By evening I will have made a few marks on paper
and put them in a place where you might find them.

Runway

A November blackbird doesn't relinquish her seat
from an aeroplane's wing.

Content to skywatch a while, her bead-stubborn eye
pierces the tail end of a cloud racing.

As if she came from a courtyard centuries back,
the wet air, the soon-to-be lit dark;

little gypsy, little pirate:
O, to have that ear and eye.

Acknowledgements

'That Heron' appeared in *Eamon at 80: Celebrating Eamon Grennan* (The Gallery Press, 2022).

The author thanks Peter, Jean, Suella and Anne — all that love for books.